ROLLERDANCEMAN
THE BIOGRAPHY OF RICHARD HUMPHREY

CARLA DOMETRIUS

Rollerdanceman: The Biography of Richard Humphrey

Copyright © 2020 by Carla Dometrius

Illustrations copyright © by Aimee Stevland

Illustration on page 1 © by David Harrison

Photo on page 25 copyright © by Beto Lopez

Other photos courtesy of the Richard Humphrey Collection

Patson Media
San Francisco

For my fourth-grade teacher, Scott Rombokas, who brought the stories of great people to life. - CD

Contents

Skaters Take to the Stage 1

It's a Boy! 4

On the Move 10

Roller Skating Hits the Streets 13

Skating Opens Doors 20

Something New 24

More Opportunities 30

Learn "Long" 36

Glossary of Terms 40

Acknowledgements 42

Skaters Take to the Stage

The audience applauds as Richard rolls out to meet the camera and joins Dr. Oz, in front of his viewers. Dr. Mehmet Oz, the host of the show, who waits on the stage in his new "No Strings Attached" skates, is ready to learn to roller dance.

The popular television host is trying to find different ways to fulfill the challenge of 10,000 steps per day. He explains to his studio and television audience that although he has never roller skated before, he is looking forward to learning how to dance in skates. After Richard is introduced, he shows Dr. Oz the steps to the dance that he has specifically **choreographed** for this occasion.

From "The Cowboy" to "The Shimmy," Oz catches on quickly. Soon they are joined on stage by New York's own Sisters in Motion skate dance crew. Led by Tanya Dean, this group was formed to bring unity to women in skating. Before long, everyone on stage is roller dancing to what would become known as the "Oz Dance."

You can learn this dance by visiting https://youtu.be/VKyUyEI0gMw.

It's a Boy!

On a beautiful first day of October, in 1952, Horace and Ocie Humphrey welcomed their new baby Richard to the world. Horace was a construction worker who also worked as a cab driver, while Ocie earned money as a server and cook. The family lived in San Francisco's Fillmore District. The next year, Kenneth would enter the world, and before long they would be joined by two girls: Patricia and then Katherine. A few years later, little Victor would complete the family.

The Humphreys loved physical activities, and the children were encouraged to participate in many sports. Richard's home was always bustling with activity. The siblings learned to bowl and play basketball and tennis. Soon roller skating would enter the picture.

When Richard was 5 years old, he received his first pair of roller skates. These skates were very different from modern ones. During the late 1950s, skates had a metal plate with wheels that clipped onto the bottom of shoes. They were then tightened by a key.

Many of the children in the Fillmore had roller skates. Friends skated on the sidewalk, chasing one another and rolling around the neighborhood.

Richard also loved bowling. He often went to the local bowling alley with friends. It was during this time that Richard learned about how practice and hard work can improve skills. His bowling game got even better, and in 1964 his name was mentioned in the *Sun Register*. He was only 11, and the paper reported on him because, even at this age, he was already reaching high scores in the league.

One day, Richard was keeping score for some older bowlers. A man from the neighborhood, Gervis Bookman, nicknamed Sugarman, invited young Rich to the skating rink. Richard asked Ocie if he could go, and though he went, it would be years before skating became a priority.

Richard had many other hobbies and focused his energy on tennis, basketball, and racquetball. By the time he was 15, the Humphrey home was becoming quite crowded, and Richard decided to move across town to live with his godparents.

On the Move

Richard took up table tennis and enrolled at Woodrow Wilson High School. While attending high school, he excelled in track and field activities, including the 100-meter dash, 120-yard relay, hurdles, long jump, and high jump. His team reigned in an all-city undefeated season during his senior year. It was because of his swiftness that Richard's godfather gave him the nickname "Speed."

It was also during this time that Richard met a young woman named Jean. The two dated in high school, and after graduating in 1970, they were married. Four years later, their son Damon was born. Damon weighed only 1 lb., 10 oz. at birth and was later diagnosed with mild **spina bifida**. Though it was a scary time, Damon grew strong. Richard passed along his love of sports to his son. The two of them often spent time with one another engaged in bowling or riding bicycles.

Roller Skating Hits the Streets

1979 gave rise to the perfected polyurethane wheel, and it was now being mass-produced in factories. The material had been recently employed by Frank Nasworthy to improve wheels for skateboarders. This special wheel revolutionized the world of roller skating and enabled people to skate outdoors longer and more comfortably. The increased mobility of the wheel helped popularize skating and made the sport accessible to everyone.

This new craze caught on like wildfire, and San Francisco's Golden Gate Park was teeming with energy. John F. Kennedy Drive, just inside the park, was the area's hub for roller skating. Many streets were closed to car traffic, and skate rental vans lined both sides of JFK Drive. For only $1, locals and tourists alike could roll through the park all day.

The media was also interested in this popular sport. Saul Zaentz, who had produced the 1978 animated version of *Lord of the Rings*, filmed a **pilot** for a series called *Dancing Wheels*. Richard and other skaters were invited to be a part of this new show, where they would perform tricks, splits, and a showcase of dance steps. Sadly, after filming the pilot, the series never made it to television.

Richard was inspired by a New York skating pioneer, Bill Butler, whom he had read about in a 1979 magazine called *Rollerskating*. Butler was doing something different, and this motivated Richard. Together with friends DeWayne McDaniels and Wayne Evans, Richard formed a group called the Golden Rollers.

The three men worked and skated together, perfecting their craft and becoming popular for the "Alpha Kick," splits on skates, and the dance that would eventually be known in skate dance circles as the "#1." They were so entertaining that many people came to Golden Gate Park just to watch this talented trio.

The Golden Rollers grew to be local celebrities. In 1982, they were even featured in *Evening Mag*, a television series spot-lighting people and places of interest in San Francisco. In 1983, the Golden Rollers also appeared on the popular Emmy-nominated television show, *Real People*.

When the director of San Francisco's Smuin Ballet, Michael Smuin, saw Richard skate, he and others were invited to perform in front of thousands at San Francisco's War Memorial Opera House. Richard even performed as an opening act for comedians Ronny Schell and Phyllis Diller.

Skating Opens Doors

Richard's marriage to Jean ended. In 1985, he married Beverly. A couple of years later, his son Neil was born. Richard enjoyed spending time with his son, and soon Richard introduced Neil to table tennis. With his dad's help, Neil also learned to skate and ride a bike. The two even played trumpet together!

Many people were interested in learning to dance on skates, so Richard started giving roller dance lessons at Le Park, a San Francisco roller rink where he worked as Skating Director. Le Park was a converted warehouse with a waterfall inside. Richard worked there as a disc jockey (or DJ) and taught skating four days a week. It was during this time that one of his students invited him to Sao Paolo, Brazil.

Richard considered himself very lucky to be able to take this trip. He packed his bags quickly and flew to Brazil. This was a once in a lifetime vacation, and he was able to see many beautiful sights, as well as perform two roller skating demonstrations.

Eventually, Le Park closed. For many years, this was the last indoor roller rink in San Francisco. Across the nation, other roller rinks suffered the same fate as a new roller-craze began to catch on with the public.

Something New

The first commercially available **in-line** skates appeared in 1988. As the popularity of in-lines rose, **quad** skating noticed a marked decline in popularity. But this did not change Richard's love for skating. Even though he eventually warmed up to in-line skates and agreed to give lessons to those wishing to learn how to skate in them, he was still committed to the classic quad skate.

Richard began giving lessons at a studio in San Francisco's Mission District called Third Wave Dance Studios. Richard had around fifteen dedicated students, and he continued to teach there for three years.

Richard always had varied interests. This applied to his **affinity** for classic car restoration. Back in 1978, he had bought a 1960 classic truck. Then, in 1989, he attended his first classic car show. This has remained one of his interests ever since.

Around this time, he also created his own roller dance workout for VHS (Video Home System or video cassette), which came complete with a step-by-step booklet. This is still available in DVD form on his website:

www.rollerdance.com

Richard split with his wife, Beverly, in 1990. It was then that he found a new pastime: designing artwork for bowling shirts. He enjoyed this new hobby so much that he expanded and began creating art for other sports. He even started his own company called Movement in Motion. The idea behind the designs was to create art with images where, in Richard's words, he is "able to catch the movement in action."

By 1995, he was offering lessons from the Jon Sims studio in the city's Mission District. Richard and his students were invited to perform at an Oakland Skates hockey team half-time show. He choreographed and "called" steps to his students, including 8-year-old prodigy Melanie Miles (daughter of San Francisco's Godfather of Skate, David Miles). The audience enjoyed this entertaining break in the middle of the game.

Richard's skill for creating skate dances became widely known in the skating community, and even Olympic Gold Medalist ice skater Kristi Yamaguchi sought him out to help her with choreography.

By this time, Richard had remarried. His new wife was named Diann. They had met a few years before and had gotten along well - enjoying walking, exploring, and spending time together.

Always looking for a new way to workout, in 1998, Richard turned to golf. He found this sport to be humbling, and he averaged a couple of days at the golf course per week. Richard enjoyed the challenge of this sport and currently continues to hit the green at least once a week.

In 1999, Richard received a patent for his own creation: The Rollerdeck Plus Fitness Machine. This product, which is a self-contained skate floor and upper body workout system, provides a portable floor for skaters on the go. With this piece of equipment, a skater can have a full-body workout anywhere.

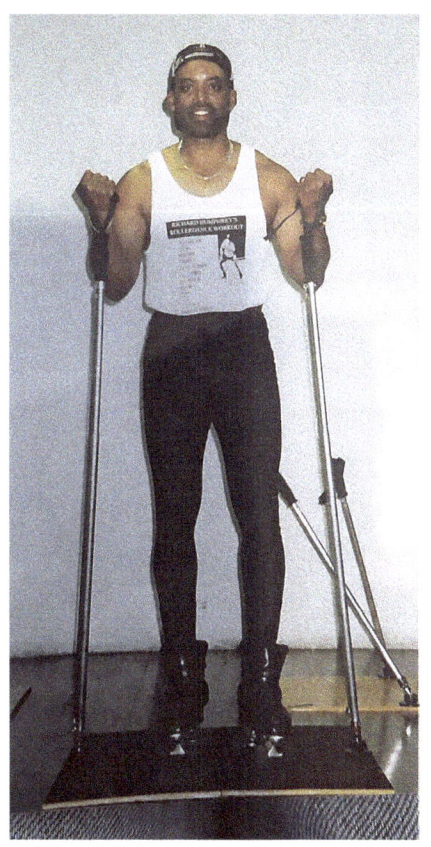

More Opportunities

In October 2006, Richard was featured in the "Body Talk" section of *Ebony*, a magazine that focuses on lifestyles of African Americans. In this spread, he discussed the many health benefits of roller skating for all ages and fitness levels.

The article also talked about the Quadline skate. This is a skate created by Skates.com in response to Richard's **agility** on his quad skates. The idea behind the Quadline is that, because of its bigger wheels, one can skate even faster and increase cardio levels more easily (which stimulates the heart and helps with fitness).

Later that same year, Richard was contacted by actor and comedian Damon Wayans to do skate stunts as his double in an episode of his series *The Underground*. In this episode, Wayans was asked about what he liked to do to unwind and keep his mental health strong. From the psychologist's office, producers cut to a scene of Damon "roll bouncing" at his local skating rink. Richard wore identical clothing to Damon, and the producers did a Hollywood trick by connecting the scenes together, making it look like Wayans was doing all the skating himself.

In 2009, the Humphrey skate boot **debuted**. It was manufactured by the well-known skate company Reidell. The skate was the first one in Riedell's 60 years to be made with no laces. They called it "No Strings Attached."

Along with his boot, Rollerbones released the Golden Rollerbones Richard Humphrey signature wheel. This wheel was designed with the assistance of Lee Cole, another San Francisco skater, who was the founder of the skate shop, Skates on Haight.

All the years of sports had finally taken their toll on Richard's knees. In the years of 2016 and 2017, Richard had knee replacement surgery on both knees. After **rehabilitation**, and a few months of being unable to skate, Richard was skating, bowling, and golfing once again.

Following Richard's knee replacement, he began teaching at Rollerdance Academy. Richard taught all levels on Sunday mornings in this brightly lit studio in the Dogpatch District. Sadly though, due to sharp increases in rent, the studio had to shut down. This opened the door to Richard teaching at City Dance.

During the Coronavirus pandemic, Richard continued to give lessons. When the pandemic was in its early stages, Richard taught virtually on Zoom. His students joined each class with their computers as Richard instructed from inside his home. By the summer, when social restrictions were temporarily lifted, Rollerdance Academy students met with Richard at Washington Park in Alameda. There they learned dances with masks on, six feet apart.

Richard continues to teach classes on Sundays. You can find the information for his current venue on his web page:

    rollerdance.com

After teaching his morning class, you will likely find Richard at 6th Avenue Skatin' Place on a Sunday afternoon. He will teach his craft to anyone who is interested and hopes to pass down his dance moves, including "Long," "Short," and "Regular." These are some of the most popular skate moves around the world, and they have been modified and imitated by many new skaters.

Learn "Long"

Here is Richard's most popular dance. It is a little like a grapevine pattern. Practice this, and you can join in on the line dancing at 6th Avenue, or maybe you can be the one to take this move to your own local skate spot or roller rink.

Start by rolling the right skate up onto its heel.

Then cross the left foot in front of the right; at the same time, roll the right skate back a little.

Then roll the right foot forward again. Roll the left skate behind the right.

Roll the left skate forward onto its heel.

Now cross the right skate in front of the left, and reverse the grapevine pattern in the opposite direction. Continue to the left, and repeat for as long as you like.

If you are with other people, someone may want to "call" a variation of "Long" or a different move.

There are many other skate dance steps that can be connected to "Long." A move that is closely related and goes well in a sequence is "Regular." Both steps can be found on Richard's YouTube page under "The Hookup." Type this web address in your browser to locate:

https://youtu.be/aJjn8ZQLpbY

Glossary of Terms

choreographed – created the sequence of steps and moves for a performance of dance.

spina bifida – a defect of the spine in which part of the spinal cord and its membranes are exposed through a gap in the backbone. It can cause legs to be unable to move or cause problems in the brain.

pilot – a television program made to test viewers' reaction with characters and plot for a series.

in-lines – skates with two to five wheels arranged in a straight row from front to back. Some have a rubber brake in the back used for stopping.

quads – four-wheeled roller skates that have two wheels in the front and two in the back on each skate. Sometimes they have a rubber brake, or toe stop, in the front to use for stopping (many serious dance skaters usually do not have this feature because the brake can get in the way of the more advanced dance moves).

affinity – a special attraction to something.

agility – the ability to move with ease.

debuted – presented to the public.

rehabilitation – Returning to a former state of fitness after rest, training, and therapy.

variation – similar, with many shared characteristics.

sequence – a set of steps in an order that can be repeated.

Acknowledgements

Thank you to Gerald Johnson for the companionship and for teaching me to be an alert skater.

Also, I am grateful for my editor and publisher, David Harrison, whose advice and sharp eye for aesthetics made this book a reality and whose skating dog Minnie brings joy to all who meet her.

Additionally, I appreciate my son Holden for his positive spirit, willingness to try new things, and comradery during our early skating experiences.

Thank you to Aimee Bruckner for agreeing to contribute the illustrations for *Rollerdanceman*.

To David Miles and family, I am filled with gratitude for all the skating opportunities, the encouragement to learn street skating, and the inspiration to seek my skate instructor certification.

A special thanks to Laura Sunday and Richard Humphrey for giving me skates and teaching me to dance.

Many thanks to my students at San Francisco Pacific Academy for listening to this book from its earliest conception and offering pure constructive criticism.

Most importantly, I recognize Carl Cates, whose work ethic and many sacrifices taught me perseverance so that I have the fortitude to finish projects.

www.ingramcontent.com/pod-product-compliance
Lightning Source LLC
Chambersburg PA
CBHW042122100526
44587CB00025B/4153